Elevation Church
11416 E. Independence Blvd., Suite N
Matthews, NC 28105

Design: Sophie Smith
Art: Julius Shumpert

Printed in the United States of America

First Printing, 2022

ISBN 978-1-7377604-2-9

www.ImmeasurablyMore.com

IMMEASURABLY MORE

A Word Study with the Book of Ephesians

AN ELEVATION CHURCH STUDY WITH HOLLY FURTICK
WRITTEN BY BRITTANY AKINSOLA AND ERIC STANFORD

"Now to him who is able to do immeasurably more than all we ask or imagine, according to his power that is at work within us, to him be glory in the church and in Christ Jesus throughout all generations, for ever and ever! Amen.

EPHESIANS 3:20-21

Table of Contents

A Welcome from Holly

If I had to say which passage of scripture I've heard my husband quote the most, I think it would have to be Ephesians 3:20-21: *"Now to him who is able to do immeasurably more than all we ask or imagine, according to his power that is at work within us, to him be glory in the church and in Christ Jesus throughout all generations, for ever and ever! Amen."*

He used it as a core teaching when our church was just getting started, he preached sermons on it to stir our faith, and has quoted it as a benediction to close our services more times than I can count. This verse is a foundational truth of Elevation Church. It is in our bones.

And yet, I still don't know if our human minds are even capable of grasping these verses. Our most audacious prayer requests pale in comparison to what God is able to do. His incomprehensible power is at work within us now, and it is something we can experience in every moment of our lives.

Over the next few weeks, we're going to read through the book of Ephesians and, together, we'll discover how we can experience God's power in our everyday lives.

> If you're confused and don't know what to do, God is able to supply you with *immeasurably more wisdom.*

> If you've been telling yourself God can't accept you or that you don't have anything to offer, God provides *immeasurably more grace.*

> If the future frightens you or you're facing a task that seems overwhelming, God will fill you with *immeasurably more confidence.*

If you are troubled within your spirit or caught in conflict with others, God can give you *immeasurably more peace.*

If It doesn't feel as though God cares about you, or if you are struggling with relationships that aren't going well, God offers *immeasurably more love.*

If life seems too hard and the opposition too powerful, God will help you stand firm with *immeasurably more strength.*

Regardless of your past, background, or struggles you've faced, God has chosen you. He wants to do things in and through you beyond your wildest dreams and imagination. I'm excited for you to join me as we take the journey to believe God for immeasurably more in our lives. Are you ready? Let's do this!

To Him be glory throughout all generations, for ever and ever!

How to Use This Book

Immeasurably More is a Bible study about many of the promises of God found throughout scripture, and more specifically, Paul's letter to the Ephesians. Each week focuses on a single word found in scripture and is designed to help you grow in your understanding of them *(wisdom, grace, confidence, peace, love, and strength)*. By focusing on a single word, each week you will dive deeper and begin to access immeasurably more of it in your own life.

There are three weekly elements in this study book that will help you accomplish this:

GROUP TIME
You can use this study individually, but you'll get much more out of it if you do it in a group setting. Each week kicks off with group time, when you'll get to know your group members, watch a video by Holly Furtick, and start exploring Ephesians chapter by chapter. Try to be consistent in attending your group, because there's nothing that can build our faith up like being part of a small group of people who want to grow closer to God and one another.

DAILY READINGS
After group time, over the course of four days, you can use this book to dig deeper into the chapter and word your group discussed. This is when you'll examine powerful passages in God's Word, pray, reflect on challenging questions, and consider how God would want you to apply what you're learning to your life.

DAY 1
Read the assigned chapter of Ephesians and begin to apply it to your life.

DAY 2
Discover a broader understanding of each week's biblical concept and read some of the Bible's important passages on the weekly word.

DAY 3
Read and reflect on Bible stories that illustrate the weekly word, showing you what the word might look like in action in your life.

DAY 4
Read the week's key verse (which inspires the word for that week) and begin to apply it to your life so it becomes a part of your spiritual DNA.

ADDITIONAL READINGS
To help you gain a better understanding, each week has additional readings that provide more insight into the weekly word. Included in these additional readings are verses and Bible stories, historical context pieces, as well as vignettes about people who lived in or traveled through Ephesus.

For additional resources, check out ImmeasurablyMore.com or email Studies@ElevationChurch.org.

Types of Bible Versions

Why are there so many different Bible versions available? One reason is that translators have made different trade-offs between accuracy and understandability. When trying to understand a Bible passage, it can be helpful to read it in different types of Bibles and pick up different nuances. For that reason, on Day 4 of each week, we recommend you read the key verse in a couple of different translations to broaden your view and understanding of the scripture you will be memorizing.

THE THREE MAIN TYPES OF BIBLES INCLUDE:

1. *Word-for-word translations.* These Bibles stick closely to the original biblical texts, which were written in Hebrew, Aramaic, and Greek.

2. *Thought-for-thought translations.* These try to represent the meaning of the original writings with more familiar language for today's readers, such as by replacing a biblical idiom with a modern-day saying.

3. *Paraphrases.* The authors of these versions write in a more individual fashion and take more license with the language to try to make the Bible sound as if it had been written in our own day.

As examples, here are the approaches taken in a few popular Bibles:

- English Standard Version (ESV)—word for word
- New Living Translation (NLT)—thought for thought
- New International Version (NIV)—balance between word for word and thought for thought
- The Message (MSG)—paraphrase by Eugene Peterson

WHAT VERSION DOES PASTOR STEVEN FURTICK USE?
Pastor Steven usually uses the NIV when he preaches because it is a widely accepted translation that balances accuracy and understandability.

WHERE CAN I ACCESS MULTIPLE VERSIONS OF THE BIBLE?
Check out Bible Gateway online or download the YouVersion app.

HOW DO I KNOW WHAT KIND OF BIBLE I HAVE?
The translation of your Bible can be easily identified with a three- or four-letter abbreviation, such as NIV for the New International Version. With a physical Bible, this abbreviation is usually on the spine or cover of your Bible and can also be found on the title or copyright page.

Bible Translation Chart

USE THIS CHART TO IDENTIFY THE TYPE OF TRANSLATION YOUR BIBLE IS:

WORD FOR WORD | THOUGHT FOR THOUGHT | PARAPHRASE

1   2 3 4 5 6 7   8 9 10 11   12 13   14   15 16 17   18   19   20

1 NASB: New American Standard Bible
2 AMP: Amplified Bible
3 ESV: English Standard Version
4 RSV: Revised Standard Version
5 KJV: King James Version
6 NKJV: New King James Version
7 HCSB: Holman Christian Standard Bible
8 NRSV: New Revised Standard Version
9 NAB: New American Bible
10 NJB: New Jerusalem Bible

11 NIV: New International Version
12 TNIV: Today's New International Version
13 NCV: New Century Version
14 TPT: The Passion Translation
15 NLT: New Living Translation
16 NLRV: New International Reader's Version
17 GNT: Good News Translation (also Good News Bible)
18 CEV: Contemporary English Version
19 TLB: The Living Bible
20 MSG: The Message

Outline of the Letter to the Ephesians

I. OPENING (1:1–23)

Greeting (1:1–2)

Praise to God (1:3–14)
- Praise to the Father for choosing believers (1:3–6)
- Praise to the Son for redeeming believers (1:7–12)
- Praise to the Spirit for sealing believers (1:13–14)

Paul's first prayer for the Ephesians (1:15–23)
- Asking God to enlighten the Ephesians (1:15–19a)
- Describing Christ's power and authority (1:19b–23)

II. A UNITED CHURCH OF GENTILES AND JEWS (2:1–3:21)

The effects of grace for all believers (2:1–10)
- Formerly spiritually dead (2:1–3)
- Now spiritually alive (2:4–10)

The gift of peace for all believers (2:11–22)
- The former separation of Gentiles from God (2:11–12)
- The unity of Gentile and Jewish believers in Christ (2:13–22)

Paul's gospel servanthood (3:1–13)
- Revelation of the mystery of the gospel (3:1–6)
- Paul's call to preach to the Gentiles (3:7–13)

Paul's second prayer for the Ephesians (3:14–21)
- Asking God to give power and knowledge to the Ephesians (3:14–19)
- Praise to Him who can do immeasurably more (3:20–21)

III. LIVING LIKE GOD'S PEOPLE

One church (4:1–16)
- Unity through faith (4:1–6)
- Diversity through gifts and ministries (4:7–13)
- Goal: spiritual maturity (4:14–16)

Holiness (4:17–5:20)
- The spiritual darkness of the Gentiles (4:17–19)
- How the Ephesians were taught another way (4:20–24)
- Therefore, put away sin (4:25–32)
- Live a life of Christlike love (5:1–2)
- Shun immorality (5:3–7)
- Live in the light (5:8–20)

Relationships in the home (5:21–6:9)
- Submitting to one another (5:21)
- Wives and husbands (5:22–33)
- Children and parents (6:1–4)
- Slaves and masters (6:5–9)

Strength in the Lord (6:10–20)
- The armor of God (6:10–18)
- Paul's request for prayer (6:19–20)

IV. FINAL GREETINGS (6:21–24)

Paul, an Unlikely Missionary

When Jesus was a young child living in Nazareth, another Jewish boy, named Saul, was born in Tarsus, an important Roman town in what is today southern Turkey. Saul—who is better known by his Latin name, Paul—probably never met Jesus in the flesh. But Paul would arguably become a more influential apostle ("sent one") than even the disciples whom Jesus gathered about Him during His lifetime on earth. You would never have expected this if you'd met Paul as a young man.

Early in his life, Paul was very serious about his Judaism. Although he was born outside of Israel and possessed Roman citizenship, his parents were Jewish, and he may have spent much of his childhood and youth in Jerusalem. He studied under one of the most influential rabbis of his day—Gamaliel. He belonged to the legalistic Pharisee party, and

while still a young man, he was a member of the Sanhedrin, or Jewish ruling council. He later would recall, "I was advancing in Judaism beyond many of my own age among my people and was extremely zealous for the traditions of my fathers" (Galatians 1:14).

The man who would become known for his missionary journeys started out with the intention of making persecution journeys—tracking down Christian Jews who had fled Jerusalem and arresting and torturing them. But then, in about AD 35, the risen and ascended Jesus intervened, saying, "Saul, Saul, why do you persecute me?" (Acts 9:4). The persecutor of Christians became a Christian himself, stunning everybody—Paul most of all! He called himself "one abnormally born" (1 Corinthians 15:8), that is, an apostle added later and in a different way from the others.

Timeline of Paul's Life

Lines, brackets, and dotted lines help show the sequence of events but are not meant to point to precise months or days within a given year, since exact dating is difficult.

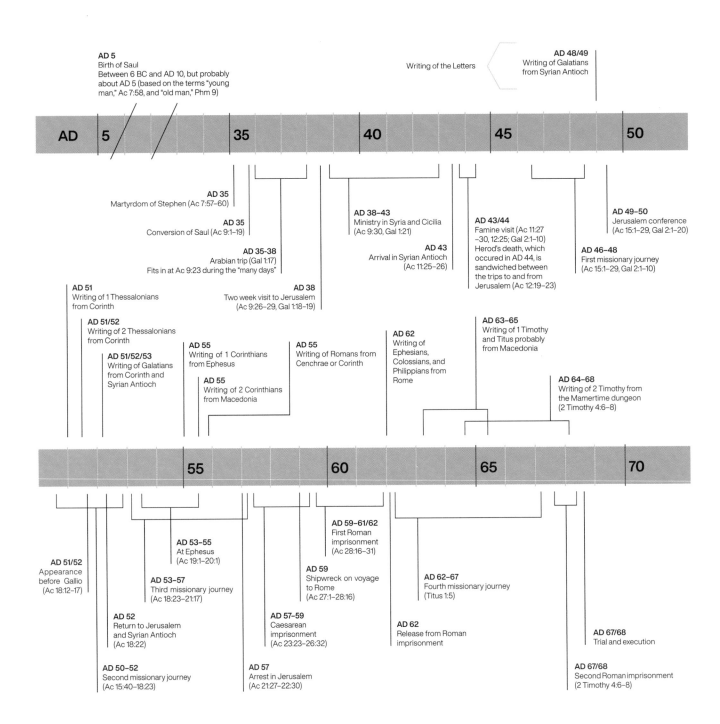

AD 5
Birth of Saul
Between 6 BC and AD 10, but probably about AD 5 (based on the terms "young man," Ac 7:58, and "old man," Phm 9)

Writing of the Letters

AD 48/49
Writing of Galatians from Syrian Antioch

AD 5 35 40 45 50

AD 35
Martyrdom of Stephen (Ac 7:57–60)

AD 35
Conversion of Saul (Ac 9:1–19)

AD 35–38
Arabian trip (Gal 1:17)
Fits in at Ac 9:23 during the "many days"

AD 38
Two week visit to Jerusalem
(Ac 9:26–29, Gal 1:18–19)

AD 38–43
Ministry in Syria and Cicilia
(Ac 9:30, Gal 1:21)

AD 43
Arrival in Syrian Antioch
(Ac 11:25–26)

AD 43/44
Famine visit (Ac 11:27–30, 12:25; Gal 2:1–10)
Herod's death, which occured in AD 44, is sandwiched between the trips to and from Jerusalem (Ac 12:19–23)

AD 46–48
First missionary journey
(Ac 15:1–29, Gal 2:1–10)

AD 49–50
Jerusalem conference
(Ac 15:1–29, Gal 2:1–20)

AD 51
Writing of 1 Thessalonians from Corinth

AD 51/52
Writing of 2 Thessalonians from Corinth

AD 51/52/53
Writing of Galatians from Corinth and Syrian Antioch

AD 55
Writing of 1 Corinthians from Ephesus

AD 55
Writing of 2 Corinthians from Macedonia

AD 55
Writing of Romans from Cenchrae or Corinth

AD 62
Writing of Ephesians, Colossians, and Philippians from Rome

AD 63–65
Writing of 1 Timothy and Titus probably from Macedonia

AD 64–68
Writing of 2 Timothy from the Mamertime dungeon (2 Timothy 4:6–8)

55 60 65 70

AD 51/52
Appearance before Gallio
(Ac 18:12–17)

AD 52
Return to Jerusalem and Syrian Antioch
(Ac 18:22)

AD 50–52
Second missionary journey
(Ac 15:40–18:23)

AD 53–55
At Ephesus
(Ac 19:1–20:1)

AD 53–57
Third missionary journey
(Ac 18:23–21:17)

AD 57
Arrest in Jerusalem
(Ac 21:27–22:30)

AD 57–59
Caesarean imprisonment
(Ac 23:23–26:32)

AD 59
Shipwreck on voyage to Rome
(Ac 27:1–28:16)

AD 59–61/62
First Roman imprisonment
(Ac 28:16–31)

AD 62–67
Fourth missionary journey
(Titus 1:5)

AD 62
Release from Roman imprisonment

AD 67/68
Trial and execution

AD 67/68
Second Roman imprisonment
(2 Timothy 4:6–8)

The Missionary Journeys of Paul

First ———

Second ———

Third ———

Rome ———

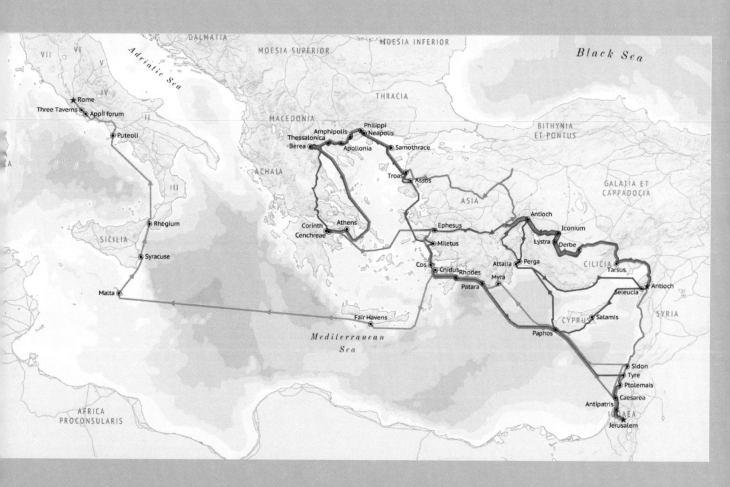

Immeasurably More *Intro*

im·meas·ur·ab·ly more *adjective phrase*

1. incapable of being measured

2. limitless

group time

As believers in Christ, we're meant to live an abundant life here on earth. This means God not only wants to meet our needs, He wants to exceed them. This week, we will begin to open our hearts to receive immeasurably more in our lives.

GET TO KNOW YOUR GROUP

Use the space below to write down the names and contact information of the members in your group, along with their specific prayer requests for immeasurably more.

video teaching notes

Can you think of a time when you asked God for one thing, but He answered with more than you could have imagined?

Which word (wisdom, grace, confidence, peace, love, strength) are you most excited to study and why?

Father, most anywhere we begin reading in Your Word, we quickly find You giving Your people not only what they need but far more than they need. As we walk through this study, please open up our hearts and help us learn to do two things, and do them well. First, help us to recall and give thanks for all the times in our lives when You've faithfully provided over and above what we've needed. Second, help us create the habit in our lives of always believing You will, whatever the circumstances, give us more of what we need.

AMEN.

day 1 Immeasurably More *Intro*

Today, you will begin to familiarize yourself with Ephesians and its author, the apostle Paul.

PRAY   God, speak to me today. Reveal Yourself to me. Amen.

READ   Page 12–15 and 21. As you learn about Ephesians and its author, Paul, take note of, highlight, or underline what stands out to you in this week's reading.

REFLECT   In your own words, what is one new insight you learned about Ephesians?

What stood out to you about the apostle Paul in this week's reading?

After reading pages 12–15 and 21, what else caught your attention?

Ephesians is a letter, and like all letters, it was originally meant to be read from start to finish. If you have time before your next group meeting, sit down and read Ephesians all the way through without stopping, just as the recipients of the letter would have read it. You'll be studying the letter chapter by chapter in the coming weeks.

WHO WROTE EPHESIANS?	The Apostle Paul
WHEN WAS THIS LETTER WRITTEN?	AD 62, while Paul was imprisoned in Rome
WHO WAS THIS LETTER WRITTEN TO?	Some of the early manuscripts of Ephesians do not contain the words "To God's holy people in Ephesus" (Ephesians 1:1), meaning this phrase may have been added later. Nor does the letter refer to any situations specific to Ephesus. So Paul may not have really written this letter to the church of Ephesus.

Most likely this was a "circular letter." In other words, Paul wrote this letter to be read, not just by the Christians of Ephesus, but also among all the churches that had been planted in that region. |

IMMEASURABLY MORE

Have you ever asked yourself questions like: What if I'm only scratching the surface of what God is trying to do through me? Are there places in my life right now that I may be limiting God? How about asking yourself this question: What would it look like if I began to believe God for immeasurably, exceedingly, abundantly more in my life?

A life-changing truth Paul prayed centuries ago can be found in our key scripture for this study, and remains true today in our lives as well: We have a God who is able to do immeasurably more than all we ask or imagine. This means we have a God who is not just trying to do the bare minimum for us, but who is openhanded and gracious to us. He not only wants to meet our needs, He wants to exceed them. Is your heart open to receiving all God has for you?

Paul's Ministry in Ephesus

The apostle Paul did an impressive amount of traveling in a day when you could get around only by foot, ship, or horse. And of all the places he visited on his ministry itinerary, the great city of Ephesus was a standout.

In about AD 52 or 53, after leaving Corinth, Paul stopped off in Ephesus on his way to Jerusalem (Acts 18:19–21). During this quick visit, Paul followed his usual strategy of going first to speak to the local Jewish community, trying to persuade them that Jesus was the Messiah and Son of God. At this point, the Ephesian Jews were intrigued enough to ask Paul to stay longer. But he stuck to his travel plans, promising, "I will come back if it is God's will" (verse 21). He left his friends Priscilla and Aquila in Ephesus to minister in his absence.

Within months, Paul was back in Ephesus. He'd decided to make this city a temporary headquarters for his ministry. One of the first things he did was straighten out the theology of a group of men who had somehow heard only about the baptism of John the Baptist, not baptism in Jesus's name (Acts 19:1–7).

Paul went back to preaching in the Ephesus synagogue, but he began getting opposition from some of the local Jews. In fact, it got so heated that he quit the synagogue and started preaching in a rented lecture hall to anyone who wanted to listen. He kept this up for two years, and it resulted in dramatic progress of the gospel (Acts 19:8–10). The miracles God was doing through Paul at this time also helped to spread his fame (verses 11-12). When some men tried to copy Paul's work as an exorcist, invoking Jesus's name without actually knowing Jesus, an evil spirit revealed their deception. This led to even greater renown for Jesus in Ephesus and the surrounding territory (verses 13–20).

While in Ephesus, Paul wrote a letter in which he stated, "I will stay on at Ephesus until Pentecost, because a great door for effective work has opened to me, and there are many who oppose me" (1 Corinthians 16:8–9). Notice there were both effective work and many who opposed. These were exciting times in the early spread of Christianity!

Paul also made the curious comment "I fought wild beasts in Ephesus" (1 Corinthians 15:32). He probably wasn't claiming that he literally had been thrown in the arena to fight a wild animal (something that did happen in Ephesus, as in other Roman cities). More likely, he was using blood sport as a metaphor for his conflicts with human opponents. Not only had the local Jews let him know he was unwelcome in their synagogue, but an even bigger conflict broke out just as Paul was making plans to move on from the city.

By this point, so many Ephesians were leaving pagan religion to follow Jesus that one of the many craftsmen who made their living off the Temple of Artemis stirred up a riot, because he feared losing his income. Thankfully, a city official restored order before violence was done, but Paul knew it was time for him to go. After spending about three years in Ephesus, Paul left behind him a much larger and more vibrant church than there had been when he arrived. Both Jews and Gentiles had become believers, and the gospel was spreading deep into Asia Minor.

day 2 Immeasurably More *Intro*

Today, you will read some doxologies found in the Bible and gain a broader understanding of this biblical concept.

DOXOLOGY

An expression of praise to God.
Doxologies in Ephesians: **2**
Ephesians 1:3; 3:20–21

Do you ever feel like you just can't help praising God—like you've *got* to say something to tell Him how great you think He is? The writers of the New Testament sometimes felt that way. And they did it in a form we call a *doxology*. A doxology is a short, spontaneous burst of praise to God. In the New Testament, a doxology usually comes at the end of a prayer, a hymn, or a section of one of Paul's letters (as is the case with the "immeasurably more" *doxology* of Ephesians 3:20–21).

Typically, a doxology has three parts:

1. An address to the one to whom the praise is given. (For example, "Now to him who is able to do immeasurably more than all we ask or imagine, according to his power that is at work within us...")

2. A word of praise, often using the Greek word *doxa*, meaning "glory." ("...to him be glory in the church and in Christ Jesus...")

3. An eternity formula. ("...throughout all generations, for ever and ever!")

Well-known doxologies include Romans 16:25–27, 1 Timothy 1:17, and Hebrews 13:20–21. Today, you will read these scriptures and write out your own doxology to praise God.

PRAY   God, speak to me through Your Word today. Reveal Yourself to me through these scriptures. Amen.

READ   Romans 16:25-27 – A praise to our wise God
                      1 Timothy 1:17 – A praise recognizing God's eternity
                      Hebrews 13:20-21 – A praise showing God as peace, resurrection and a shepherd

REFLECT   What truths did you discover about praising God that you want to remember?

                      Take a moment to praise God and write your own doxology here:

Paul in the Bible

THE LIFE OF PAUL

- **Galatians 1:11–2:21:** Paul's own account of his life
- **Acts 7:57; 8:1–3:** Paul's career as a persecutor
- **Acts 9:1–30:** Paul's conversion
- **Acts 11:25–30; 12:25:** Paul participates in a famine relief effort
- **Acts 13–14:** Paul goes on his first missionary journey
- **Acts 15:1–35:** Paul participates in the Jerusalem council
- **Acts 15:36–18:22:** Paul goes on his second missionary journey
- **Acts 18:23–21:16:** Paul goes on his third missionary journey
- **Acts 21:17–28:31:** Paul arrested, tried, and transferred to Rome

PAUL'S LETTERS

Paul not only receives a lot of attention in the book of Acts, but he also wrote thirteen of the twenty-seven books of the New Testament—around a quarter of the New Testament by length. His books contain much of the theology that Christian beliefs are based on to this day.

Letters to churches:

- Romans
- 1 Corinthians
- 2 Corinthians
- Galatians
- Ephesians
- Philippians
- Colossians
- 1 Thessalonians
- 2 Thessalonians

Pastoral letters:

- 1 Timothy
- 2 Timothy
- Titus

A personal letter:

- Philemon

im·meas·ur·ab·ly more

synonyms:
abundantly above, infinitely more, exceedingly above, above and beyond

What other phrases, words, or people come to mind when you hear the phrase *immeasurably more*?

 # Immeasurably More *Intro*

Today, you will reflect on some Bible stories that illustrate immeasurably more in action.

PRAY   God, speak to me through Your Word today. Reveal Yourself to me through these scriptures. Amen.

READ AND REFLECT   Read each of these stories and write out the insights you discover about immeasurably more.

Mark 6:30–44—Jesus feeds a large crowd

Jonah 2–3—God shows an abundance of mercy

Exodus 16:1–18—God provides for the Israelites

What is one biblical truth you've learned?

What is one thing you can do to apply this truth to your life?

Christ also hath loved
us an offering and
ning savour.
or cov.
among you.

of God,
of redemp-
n, and anger,
put away from

n, and anger,
tender-
as God for

measure.
road: these

ned of forty fu
ners of the y
was a c

use I an
ven the
use I am
e teacher
hey

one
ate that
and he shall
ing and
on the
forth:
shall
13 Tho
burnt offer
lamb of the
ing, thou

daily
nto the
ar

offering:
ng, where
trespass
e place w
20 Then
face on t
e priest
orth: an
e ga
ne

t into the u
e people
en he br
court

"Now to him who is able to do immeasurably more than all we ask or imagine, according to his power that is at work within us, to him be glory in the church and in Christ Jesus throughout all generations, for ever and ever! Amen.

EPHESIANS 3:20–21

day 4

Immeasurably More *Intro*

Today, you will read the key verses for the Immeasurably More study and take steps to commit them to memory.

PRAY   God, speak to me through Your Word today. Reveal Yourself to me through these scriptures. Amen.

READ   Ephesians 3:20–21 (NIV). Want more insight? Read Ephesians 3:20–21 in more than one translation. See page 11. *Suggestions:* ESV, NLT, MSG

REFLECT   God speaks and reveals Himself to us through His Word. What does Ephesians 3:20-21 teach you about God?

What is one practical step you can take to apply this scripture to your life?

Use this space to reflect on what God spoke to you today and write out a prayer to Him.

Write out Ephesians 3:20–21 (NIV):

Scripture Memorization Tip: To help you commit Ephesians 3:20–21 to memory, attempt to pray the scripture as a way to make the scripture personal and meaningful to you. See if you can recite this study's memory verses next time you meet with your eGroup.

immeasurably more review

Something God revealed to me about immeasurably more is:

One practical thing I plan to do to begin to access immeasurably more in my life is:

God, I acknowledge You are worthy of all honor, glory and praise, and that You truly are able to do immeasurably more than all we ask, think, or imagine. Speak to me through this study as I access the abundance You've made available to me, and give me eyes to see Your power at work within my life each day. In Jesus's name, **AMEN.**

Immeasurably More *Wisdom*

wis·dom *n.*

1. the ability to make good use of knowledge
2. ability to recognize right from wrong
3. good judgment

group time

God desires wisdom for His people, and in chapter 1 of the book of Ephesians, Paul prayed for wisdom and revelation for the people of Ephesus. This week, we will learn this blessing was not just accessible to the church of Ephesus, but we, too, have access to immeasurably more wisdom through a closer relationship with Christ.

Read Ephesians 1 out loud as a group, and jot down anything that stands out to you below.

video teaching notes

What is one area in your life where you need wisdom?

How can you practically seek God for wisdom in this area this week?

Father, Your Word tells us wisdom is a tree of life for those who embrace it and hold it tightly, and that joyful is the person who finds wisdom. As life presents us with challenges, we want to face them victoriously in Your wisdom. So we ask You for Your wisdom, in full faith that You will give it. Help us to be diligent in the things that will cultivate immeasurably more of it in our lives day by day.

AMEN.

day 1 Immeasurably More *Wisdom*

Today, you will read scripture and begin to activate it in your life.

PRAY   God, speak to me through Your Word today. Reveal Yourself to me through these scriptures. Amen.

READ   Ephesians 1 — As you read your Bible, take time to focus on what the Lord is speaking to you through this chapter. Take note of, highlight, or underline what stands out to you in this week's reading, and be on the lookout for this week's theme: *wisdom*.

REFLECT   In your own words, what is wisdom to you?

What stood out to you about wisdom in this week's reading?

After reading chapter 1 of Ephesians, what else caught your attention from these scriptures?

God is not withholding blessings from us—we have already been blessed with every spiritual blessing. However, sometimes we lack the insight, wisdom, and relationship with God needed to receive and access the blessings He has freely given us.

Paul prayed for wisdom so his readers would know God better. You can't simply read a biography about a person and think you know them. It takes relationship and time to know someone, and this same principle applies to our relationship with Christ. What you're doing right now—studying, praying, reflecting, and meditating on who God is—is developing wisdom in you.

Below are twelve people called "wise" in the Bible. Allow these people to serve as helpful models in your own pursuit of wisdom.

ACTS 7:10	Joseph	*Wise leader* who helped rule Egypt through a major famine
ACTS 7:20–22	Moses	*Wise leader* who led Israel out of Egypt
EXODUS 31:1–5	Bezalel	*Wise artist* who designed and supervised the construction of the tabernacle
DEUTERONOMY 34:9	Joshua	*Wise leader* who learned from Moses and led the people into the promised land
2 SAMUEL 14:18–20	David	*Wise leader* who pushed through failure
1 SAMUEL 25:3	Abigail	*Wise wife* who managed her home wisely in spite of a mean husband
1 KINGS 3:5–14; 4:29–34	Solomon	*Wise leader* who ultimately failed to put God's wisdom into action
DANIEL 5:11–12	Daniel	*Wise counselor* who used God's wisdom to solve complex problems
MATTHEW 2:1–12	Magi	*Wise learners* who had special knowledge of God's visit to Earth
ACTS 6:1–10	Stephen	*Wise leader* who preached the gospel to the Jews
2 PETER 3:15–16	Paul	*Wise messenger* who preached the gospel to all who would listen
LUKE 2:40, 52; 1 CORINTHIANS 1:20–25	Christ	*Wise youth, wise Savior, and the wisdom of God* who lived a perfect life and died on the cross for our sins to be forgiven

MORE WISDOM

In this week's key verses, Paul was praying for wisdom for the church of Ephesus. Wisdom is more than just information or intelligence. You can be the smartest person in the world and still lack wisdom. Paul was praying for something profound that allows you to discern and act in significant ways.

One of the best ways to grow in wisdom is through Scripture. The Bible has 31,102 living, breathing verses, and every verse was put there for a purpose. There is immeasurably more wisdom at our disposal. The challenge will be to not just read and memorize scripture at a surface level but exercise wisdom as you learn what it is that God would speak to you through the scriptures, and let that fill your heart and move you to action.

People of Ephesus: Priscilla and Aquila

WISE CHRISTIAN SERVANTS

A surprising number of men and women of the New Testament either visited or lived in the city of Ephesus at some point in their lives. These included a Jewish Christian couple named Priscilla and Aquila.

Priscilla and Aquila were living in Rome when Emperor Claudius expelled Jews from that city in AD 49. So they moved eastward to the Greek city of Corinth, where the apostle Paul lived in their home for a year and a half. When Paul left Corinth to go back to Jerusalem, around AD 52, he took Priscilla and Aquila with him as far as Ephesus, where the couple stayed temporarily.

While the couple were in Ephesus, another Christian missionary showed up there: Apollos. He was a popular preacher of the day, but his knowledge of Christian theology had gaps in it. Instead of condemning Apollos or shunning him for his faults, Priscilla and Aquila graciously "invited him to their home and explained to him the way of God more adequately" (Acts 18:26). The couple then took Apollos with them back to Corinth. Because they had shared their wisdom with Apollos, he became even more effective as a preacher and leader. "He was a great help to those who by grace had believed" (verse 27).

day 2 Immeasurably More *Wisdom*

Today, you will read some of the Bible's important passages about wisdom and gain a broader understanding of this biblical concept.

WISDOM

Wisdom in the NIV Bible: **219 mentions**
Wisdom in Ephesians: **3 mentions**
Ephesians 1:8, 17; 3:10

Wisdom guides us in answering one of the great philosophical questions of humanity: *How shall we live?* The main Hebrew word for wisdom (*chokhmah*) describes how the wise man or woman gives to the things of God the same attention that other people give to worldly affairs. Wisdom largely comes through experience, so adversity and age can be contributors to wisdom.

Proverbs 8:22–23 personifies "wisdom" as God's first creation. And in the teachings of Paul, we learn that Christ is wisdom (1 Corinthians 1:24) and that the objective of wisdom is to know Christ better (Ephesians 1:17). To follow Jesus is to follow the ways of wisdom.

In a sense, the whole Bible is a presentation of wisdom. But four books of the Hebrew scriptures, namely Job, Proverbs, Song of Songs, and Ecclesiastes, along with a few of the psalms, are considered to be the Old Testament's "Wisdom Literature." In the New Testament, the book of James bears a lot of resemblance to this Old Testament literature. Today, you will read scriptures from the books of Proverbs and James to gain a better understanding of wisdom.

PRAY   God, speak to me through Your Word today. Reveal Yourself to me through these scriptures. Amen.

READ   Proverbs 11:2; 12:18; 16:16; 24:14—An assortment of key wisdom proverbs
                  James 1:5–8—How to ask for wisdom
                  James 3:13–18—Earthly "wisdom" versus heavenly wisdom

REFLECT   What are some cultural definitions of wisdom you've heard that you would say are off after gaining a broader biblical understanding of this concept?

                  What truths about wisdom did you discover that you want to remember?

Ephesus: Center of a Gospel Strategy

Early Christianity was mostly an urban movement. Missionaries traveled to major cities around the Roman Empire, planted churches in those cities, and then began taking the message of Jesus into surrounding regions. One of the clearest examples of this method of gospel spread took place in Ephesus, a large city for its time (perhaps as many as two hundred thousand people), located on the western coast of what is now Turkey.

Today, the ruins of Ephesus lie five miles inland from the Aegean Sea coast, but that's because the city's river has silted up over the years. Back in the first century, Ephesus was a busy commercial seaport as well as a hub of Greco-Roman culture.

Ancient Ephesus had all the features of a typical Roman city, including two agoras (public squares), a large outdoor theater, and a prytaneion (city hall) that contained a flame that was never allowed to go out. The Temple of Artemis on the city's outskirts was so immense and richly decorated that it made the list of the Seven Wonders of the Ancient World.

The apostle Paul stopped in Ephesus briefly on his second missionary journey, leaving his friends Aquila and Priscilla to carry on the Christian work there (Acts 18:19–21). Then Paul returned to Ephesus some months later (around AD 53) and stayed for three years (Acts 19–20). Paul declared about his time in Ephesus, "A great door for effective work has opened to me" (1 Corinthians 16:9).

After many of the Ephesian Jews rejected the gospel, Paul went daily to the lecture hall of Tyrannus to discuss Christ with Gentiles. "This went on for two years, so that all the Jews and Greeks who lived in the province of Asia heard the word of the Lord" (Acts 19:10). This was a clear example of the gospel spreading from an urban center to a wider area.

Paul left Ephesus around AD 55. Then, around seven years later, while Paul was imprisoned in Rome, he wrote his letter to the Ephesians. In his letter, Paul was building up the stronghold of the Christian faith that he had helped establish, with Ephesus at its center.

wis·dom

synonyms:
understanding, perception, insight, discernment,
omniscience, foresight

What other words, phrases or people
come to mind when you think of the word
wisdom?

day 3 Immeasurably More *Wisdom*

Today, you will read and reflect on some Bible stories that illustrate wisdom in action.

PRAY   God, speak to me through Your Word today. Reveal Yourself to me through these scriptures. Amen.

READ AND   Read each of these stories and write out the insights you discover about wisdom.
REFLECT

1 Samuel 25:2–42—A foolish husband and a wise wife

1 Kings 3:4–28—Solomon asked for and received wisdom

Matthew 7:24–27—Wisdom and foolish builders

In what area are you lacking wisdom? What is one biblical truth you've learned that can help you in this area?

What is one thing you can do to apply godly wisdom to the challenges or opportunities in your life?

"I keep asking that the God of our LORD Jesus Christ, the glorious Father, may give you the Spirit of wisdom and revelation, so that you may know him better. I pray that the eyes of your heart may be enlightened in order that you may know the hope to which he has called you, the riches of his glorious inheritance in his holy people, and his incomparably great power for us who believe."

EPHESIANS 1:17–19A

day 4 Immeasurably More *Wisdom*

Today, you will read this week's key verses and take steps to apply them to your life.

PRAY   God, speak to me through Your Word today. Reveal Yourself to me through these scriptures. Amen.

READ   Ephesians 1:17–19a (NIV). Want more insight? Read Ephesians 1:17–19a in more than one translation. See page 11. *Suggestions:* ESV, NLT, MSG

REFLECT   God speaks and reveals Himself to us through His Word. What does Ephesians 1:17–19a teach you about God?

What is one practical step you can take to apply this scripture to your life?

Use this space to reflect on what God spoke to you today and write out a prayer to Him.

Write out Ephesians 1:17–19a (NIV):

Have you memorized Ephesians 3:20-21 yet? Take a moment to write it out below:

Scripture Memorization Tip: To help you commit scripture to memory, dedicate time over the next couple of days to creating a memorization schedule to help you prioritize memorizing scripture in your daily routine. After sticking to this schedule, see if you can recite the scripture you're commiting to memory next time you meet with your eGroup.

wisdom review

Something God revealed to me about wisdom is:

One practical thing I plan to do to access immeasurably more wisdom in my life is:

God, bring these scriptures to my mind so I might meditate on them throughout the day. Help me to remember You are revealing Yourself, Your will, and Your wisdom to me constantly. Help me to tune my ears to hear Your voice throughout my day. In Jesus's name, **AMEN.**

Immeasurably More *Grace*

week 2

grace *n.*

1. God's free and unmerited favor for sinful humanity

2. God's benevolence on the undeserving

3. God's active kindness

group time

Grace is the gift of God's unexplainable favor that is expressed through His kindness to us. This week, we will spend time embracing the immeasurable grace God has freely given to each of us simply because of His love for us.

Read Ephesians 2 out loud as a group, and jot down anything that stands out to you below.

video teaching notes

Describe a time someone extended grace to you.

Is there an area of your life where you find it difficult to accept God's kindness?

BONUS: Who is someone in your life that you need to show grace to and how are you going to show God's kindness to them this week?

God, Your Word reminds us every good and perfect gift comes from You. Regardless of how distant we once were from You, because of Your saving grace, we now have a personal relationship with You. And regardless of the challenges we face in life—sometimes daily— You sustain us and empower us by Your grace. Thank You for Your unexpected, unmerited, and immeasurably more grace that flows freely to us today and every day. **AMEN.**

Immeasurably More *Grace*

Today, you will read scripture and begin to activate it in your life.

PRAY   God, speak to me through Your Word today. Reveal Yourself to me through these scriptures. Amen.

READ   Ephesians 2 — As you read your Bible, take time to focus on what the Lord is speaking to you through this chapter. Take note of, highlight, or underline what stands out to you in this week's reading, and be on the lookout for this week's theme: *grace*.

REFLECT   In your own words, what is grace to you?

What stood out to you about grace in this week's reading?

After reading chapter 2 of Ephesians, what else caught your attention from these scriptures?

God is generous and freely gives to us. His gift to us is not dependent on us earning a "reward" or being perfect—it's actually the opposite. He gives to us because of who He is, not because of who we are or aren't. This is one of the most important concepts in the Bible, and it is called the gift of grace.

What does grace do?

TITUS 2:11–12	Grace draws you into a closer relationship with Christ.
1 PETER 5:10	Grace gives you the strength to follow God and live a good and faithful life.
ROMANS 3:23–24	Grace blesses you, regardless of your shortcomings.
2 TIMOTHY 1:9	Grace qualifies you for what you otherwise would be unqualified for.
2 CORINTHIANS 12:9	Grace will fill the gap for your shortcomings.

MORE GRACE

Paul began his letter declaring grace for the people of Ephesus and praying they might know the riches of this grace. In this week's chapter, Paul deals directly with the theme of grace, describing it as a free gift that Christ gives to both Jews and Gentiles who believe in Him. You have access to this same gift, and it's already at work in your life today.

Have you thanked God lately for the ways He has freely blessed you? Exercise gratitude and thank Him for the ways He has extended His grace to you today.

People of Ephesus: Paul

A PICTURE OF GRACE

The great turning point in the apostle Paul's life was his conversion to faith in Jesus, described no fewer than five times in scripture (Acts 9:1–30; 22:1–21; 26:1–23; 1 Corinthians 15:1–11; Galatians 1:11–24). Paul's conversion story emphasizes that he started out as a religious legalist and zealous persecutor of the church. While he was on the road to Damascus to expand his persecution efforts, Jesus struck him down and temporarily blinded him. Later, he was filled with the Holy Spirit and commissioned to preach Jesus to the world.

After this dramatic conversion and display of grace, several years passed, about which we don't know much of Paul's activities. He spent part of that time in his hometown of Tarsus and part of it in Arabia, and he took a trip to Jerusalem. He may have worked as a tentmaker. We don't have any knowledge that he was ever married or had children. He did, however, have members of his biological family who he kept in touch with.

Then, around AD 46, having been called by God as an apostle to the Gentiles, he began a series of missionary journeys into Gentile (non-Jewish) areas. The book of Acts records three missionary journeys, during the second of which, in about AD 52 or 53, Paul first visited Ephesus. He returned a few months later to spend three years in this city.

In about AD 57, Paul was arrested in Jerusalem. He appealed his case to Caesar, and his imprisonment was nearing an end in AD 62 when he wrote the letter to the Ephesians. It's evident Paul eagerly told this story to non-Christians as a challenge for them to consider trusting in Christ themselves, and to Christians as a reminder of Christ's amazing grace.

day 2 Immeasurably More *Grace*

Today, you will read some of the Bible's important passages about grace and gain a broader understanding of this biblical concept.

GRACE

Grace in the NIV Bible: **124 mentions**

Grace in Ephesians: **11 mentions**

Ephesians 1:2, 6–8; 2:5, 7–8; 3:2, 7–8; 4:7; 6:24

The New Testament word for grace is *charis*. It is often defined as "the unmerited favor of God." In other words, it's a gift. We haven't done anything to earn it. Ephesians 2 could not be clearer about the free nature of grace. We didn't deserve it, because we were spiritually dead, subjects of the devil, interested only in gratifying our own desires, and headed for judgment. But if we have trusted in Christ, then out of His love and mercy, He has raised us to new life. "For it is by grace you have been saved, through faith—and this is not from yourselves, it is the gift of God—not by works, so that no one can boast" (verses 8-9).

Paul is not suggesting that good works are not important. In fact, he goes on immediately to say, "For we are his workmanship, created in Christ Jesus for good works, which God prepared beforehand, that we should walk in them" (verse 10 ESV). But scripture makes it clear that it would be a mistake to think works can do anything to earn us God's grace. And so there is no limit to the gratitude we should have for salvation in Christ.

PRAY   God, speak to me through Your Word today. Reveal Yourself to me through these scriptures. Amen.

READ   John 1:1–17—Grace through Jesus
Romans 5:12–21—God's abundant provision of grace
2 Corinthians 12:9—God's grace is sufficient

REFLECT   What are some cultural definitions of grace you've heard that you would say are off after gaining a broader biblical understanding of this concept?

What truths about grace did you discover that you want to remember?

Grace for All People

In a prophecy God gave to Isaiah several centuries before Jesus was born, He addressed the Servant of the Lord (the coming Messiah) in this way:

It is too small a thing for you to be my servant
> to restore the tribes of Jacob
> and bring back those of Israel I have kept.
I will also make you a light for the Gentiles,
> that my salvation may reach to the ends of the earth. (49:6)

The word Gentiles originally meant "nations," and later came to mean "non-Jews." Isaiah's prophecy, then, is a beautiful picture of the expansion of God's grace beyond the Jewish people to the whole world. And yet, when Jesus came to fulfill this prophecy, it was almost more than many Jews could accept. Why?

For centuries, the Jews had ingrained in them the idea that they were God's chosen people (Deuteronomy 7:6). To have this special relationship with God, you had to be a descendant of Abraham, Isaac, and Jacob, with circumcision as the most basic sign of belonging to the covenant community (Genesis 17). Furthermore, full acceptance by God, most Jews believed, depended on obedience to the law of Moses.

Then suddenly, after the pouring out of the Holy Spirit at Pentecost, God started doing a new thing—giving the gift of saving faith in Jesus to Gentiles. It was a big change, and for many Jews, it required a difficult adjustment in mindset.

In fact, it took a special vision from God, around AD 37, for the apostle Peter to realize God welcomed Gentiles as well as Jews (Acts 10–11). Peter testified, "I now realize how true it is that God does not show favoritism but accepts from every nation the one who fears him and does what is right" (10:34–35).

In the year 49 or 50, the church held a council in Jerusalem to reach an agreement on what the relationship between Gentile Christians and Jewish tradition should be. The final decision was simply to ask the Gentiles to avoid a few of the behaviors that would be most offensive to Jews. In other words, the council's judgment preserved the doctrine of salvation by faith.

Ethnic and religious tensions between Jewish Christians and Gentile Christians would continue for a long time. Paul hated the division between the two wings of the church, and he knew it was unnecessary and wrong. In the letter of Ephesians, he made perhaps his most eloquent statement about the breadth of grace and the unity it brings: "[Christ Jesus] himself is our peace, who has made the two groups one and has destroyed the barrier, the dividing wall of hostility, by setting aside in his flesh the law with its commands and regulations. His purpose was to create in himself one new humanity out of the two, thus making peace, and in one body to reconcile both of them to God through the cross, by which he put to death their hostility" (2:14–16).

grace

synonyms:
favor, mercy, kindness, compassion, forgiveness, undeserving

What other words, phrases or people come to mind when you think of the word *grace?*

day 3 Immeasurably More *Grace*

Today, you will read and reflect on some Bible stories that illustrate grace in action.

PRAY   God, speak to me through Your Word today. Reveal Yourself to me through these scriptures. Amen.

READ AND REFLECT   Read each of these stories and write out the insights you discover about grace.

Joshua 2; 6:22–25; Matthew 1:5—A prostitute was protected, and by grace, became a part of the lineage of Jesus

1 Samuel 16:1–13—A shepherd boy was anointed to be king, as we are anointed by the Holy Spirit for the ministries to which God calls us

Hosea 3—Hosea offered grace to an adulterous wife, as God offers grace to unfaithful people like us

In what area are you lacking grace? What is one biblical truth you've learned that can help you in this area?

What is one thing you can do to apply godly grace to the challenges or opportunities in your life?

"It is by grace you have been saved, through faith—and this is not from yourselves, it is the gift of God—not by works, so that no one can boast."

EPHESIANS 2:8–9

day 4   Immeasurably More *Grace*

Today, you will read this week's key verses and take steps to apply them to your life.

PRAY   God, speak to me through Your Word today. Reveal Yourself to me through these scriptures. Amen.

READ   Ephesians 2:8–9 (NIV). Want more insight? Read Ephesians 2:8–9 in more than one translation. See page 11. *Suggestions:* ESV, NLT, MSG

REFLECT   God speaks and reveals Himself to us through His Word. What does Ephesians 2:8–9 teach you about God?

What is one practical step you can take to apply this scripture to your life?

Use this space to reflect on what God spoke to you today and write out a prayer to Him.

Write out Ephesians 2:8–9 (NIV):

Have you memorized Ephesians 3:20-21 yet? Take a moment to write it out below:

Scripture Memorization Tip: To help you commit scripture to memory, write out the scripture ten times. See if you can recite the scripture you're commiting to memory the next time you meet with your eGroup.

grace review

Something God revealed to me about grace is:

One practical thing I plan to do to access immeasurably more grace in my life is:

God, thank You for the undeserved grace You've freely given to me. You are so loving and so generous. Help me not to take Your grace for granted and to operate fully in the grace You've given me. In Jesus's name, **AMEN.**

Immeasurably More *Confidence*

con·fi·dence *n.*

1. the feeling or belief that one can rely on
   someone or something
2. being sure of something; without a doubt
3. firm trust

group time

In chapters 1–3 of Ephesians, Paul was lifting the lid of a treasure chest full of God's blessings, promises, and plans for His people. This week, you'll learn you have access to immeasurably more confidence to approach God, knowing He is for you and has good plans for your life.

Read Ephesians 3 out loud as a group, and jot down anything that stands out to you below.

video teaching notes

What has God given me that I am tempted to diminish?

What gap do you need God's grace for in your life right now?

Father, Your Word reminds us we were first Your idea before we were our parents' idea and that Your loving plans for us existed long before we took our first breaths. Help us remember the overflowing well of confidence that is ours to draw from because of who You say we are and what we have in Christ. **AMEN.**

Immeasurably More *Confidence*

Today, you will read scripture and begin to activate it in your life.

PRAY God, speak to me through Your Word today. Reveal Yourself to me through these scriptures. Amen.

READ Ephesians 3 — As you read your Bible, take time to focus on what the Lord is speaking to you through this chapter. Take note of, highlight, or underline what stands out to you in this week's reading, and be on the lookout for this week's theme: *confidence*.

REFLECT In your own words, what is confidence to you?

What stood out to you about confidence in this week's reading?

After reading chapter 3 of Ephesians, what else caught your attention from these scriptures?

For three chapters, Paul described the blessings and promises that are yours through your relationship with God, giving you every reason to approach Him with confidence, knowing He has already accepted you and will not reject you. Have you received these promises yet, or read them and moved on?

Below are many of the blessings you've read about so far in Ephesians. Circle or highlight the ones that stand out to you. Go back and read those verses for yourself and spend time meditating on them so you can confidently receive all He's promised to you.

EPHESIANS 1:3	You are blessed with every spiritual blessing in Christ.
EPHESIANS 1:4	You are holy and blameless.
EPHESIANS 1:5–6	You are adopted as God's child.
EPHESIANS 1:7	Your sins are taken away, and you are forgiven.
EPHESIANS 1:11	You have an inheritance and a purpose.
EPHESIANS 1:13	You belong to God through the presence of the Holy Spirit.
EPHESIANS 2:6	You have been raised up to sit with Christ in heavenly realms.
EPHESIANS 2:10	You are God's handiwork.
EPHESIANS 2:13	You have been brought near to God.
EPHESIANS 3:6	You share in the promise of blessings through Christ.
EPHESIANS 3:12	You can come into God's presence with freedom and confidence.

MORE CONFIDENCE

God created us in His image, making Him the greatest source for supplying our needs, including our confidence. Psalm 118:8 tells us, "It is better to trust in the LORD than to put confidence in man" (KJV). You don't go to the grocery store looking to get an oil change. Similarly, going to the wrong place to get our confidence will lead to the wrong outcome.

If we're looking to ourselves or others, we will never be completely confident, because God is our true source and provider. Time with God, the One who made us, called us, saved us, and continues to keep us, is the best confidence booster we can access.

People of Ephesus: Tychicus, Silas, and Timothy

ENCOURAGED IN CONFIDENCE

The apostle Paul believed in the team approach to ministry. When you read the book of Acts and Paul's letters, you see he often had at least two partners traveling with him or was dispatching members of his entourage to be couriers of his mail or delegates of his authority.

We've already seen that Paul took Priscilla and Aquila with him from Corinth to Ephesus and left them there to continue ministering in his absence. In addition, the apostle caused at least three other ministry partners to go to Ephesus.

TYCHICUS was the man who brought the Ephesians letter to the province of Asia (Ephesians 6:21–22) as well as the letters of Philemon and Colossians to Colossae (Colossians 4:7). Because he is mentioned alongside "Trophimus the Ephesian" (Acts 20:4; 21:29), it is thought Tychicus was probably a native of Ephesus too. Paul called him a "dear brother and faithful servant in the Lord" (Ephesians 6:21).

SILAS (also known as Silvanus) was a prophet and a leader of the Jerusalem church who was entrusted with bearing an important message to early Gentile converts (Acts 15:22–27). Silas was also a last-minute substitute added to the team going on Paul's second missionary journey (verses 39–40).

Although the Bible doesn't specifically mention whether Silas was still with Paul when he went to Ephesus, that was probably the case.

TIMOTHY may have been Paul's dearest and most important assistant. The son of a Jewish mother and a Greek father, Timothy most likely came to faith in Jesus during Paul's visit to Timothy's hometown of Lystra, located in the interior of Asia Minor (modern-day Turkey). In both of the two biblical letters that Paul wrote Timothy, he called the younger man his spiritual son (1 Timothy 1:2; 2 Timothy 1:2).

The New testament contains many references to Timothy accompanying Paul or going places on Paul's behalf. In one case, a few years after Paul left Ephesus, the apostle sent Timothy there with the mission of confronting some false teaching that had worked its way into the church of Ephesus (1 Timothy 1:3–7).

Although Timothy was one of Paul's most trusted ministry partners, Paul felt a need to tell Timothy not to be timid or ashamed of the gospel (2 Timothy 1:7–8). Like us, Timothy needed encouragement to live in the confidence Jesus provides.

Immeasurably More *Confidence*

Today, you will read some of the Bible's important passages about confidence and gain a broader understanding of this biblical concept.

CONFIDENCE

Confidence in the NIV Bible: **37 mentions**
Confidence in Ephesians: **1 mention**
Ephesians 3:12

This week's key verse, Ephesians 3:12, says, "In [Christ Jesus] and through faith in him we may approach God with freedom and confidence." Think about what a shocking statement this must have been to its first readers.

The Hebrew word for "holy" means "set apart." Jewish people of Paul's day had a strong sense of the separation between righteousness and unrighteousness, and especially between God and people. The temple of Jerusalem was arranged by zones of access, symbolically setting apart God's holy presence from sinful humanity. Only Jews could enter the outer court of the Israelites. Inside that court was the Court of Priests, where at certain times selected priests could enter the Holy Place to tend the lamp and put out sacrificial bread. Behind a curtain was the Most Holy Place, where no one was allowed to enter except a high priest, and he could only enter once a year on the Day of Atonement. It was in the Most Holy Place the glory of the Lord dwelled.

All this takes proper account of God's otherness, His holiness. But that separation had to be broken through if we sinful humans were ever to be brought near to God. We didn't have the power to break through...so God Himself did it for us. The Father sent Jesus—God in the flesh—to dwell among us (John 1:14). At His death, the curtain blocking off the Most Holy Place was ripped from top to bottom (Matthew 27:51). What does that mean? It means now "we have confidence to enter the Most Holy Place by the blood of Jesus, by a new and living way opened for us through the curtain, that is, his body" (Hebrews 10:19–20).

Because of Christ, we are welcomed into God's presence, where we can ask whatever we want of Him—not cringing but confident, not bashful but bold.

PRAY　　　　　God, speak to me through Your Word today. Reveal Yourself to me through these scriptures. Amen.

READ　　　　　Philippians 3:1–14—Confidence in faith, not in the flesh
2 Timothy 1:6–14—Confidence in the gospel
Hebrews 4:14–16; 10:19–23—The confidence to approach God

REFLECT　　　What are some cultural definitions of confidence you've heard that you would say are off after gaining a broader biblical understanding of this concept?

What truths about confidence did you discover that you want to remember?

A Superlative Letter

Paul deliberately composed his letter to the Ephesians as a grand, soaring piece of writing, full of inspiring truths and superlative descriptions. We are blessed with every spiritual blessing in Christ. God makes available his incomparably great power for us who believe. Christ fills everything in every way. Paul preached the boundless riches of Christ. The Lord's love is wide and long and high and deep. The Father is over all and through all and in all. Our goal is to attain to the whole measure of the fullness of Christ. The fruit of the light consists in all goodness, righteousness, and truth. The church is to present herself to Christ without stain or wrinkle or any other blemish. We are to pray on all occasions with all kinds of prayers and requests.

Most famously of all, embedded at the midpoint of this letter is a doxology (outburst of praise to God) that Christians have loved to quote ever since Paul first wrote it. Ephesians 3:20-21 is a superlative of superlatives: "Now to him who is able to do immeasurably more than all we ask or imagine, according to his power that is at work within us, to him be glory in the church and in Christ Jesus throughout all generations, for ever and ever! Amen."

Because of Christ, we have confidence to approach God and ask what we want. That's amazing enough. But on top of that, God is going to do even greater things than we could think to ask!

con·fi·dence

synonyms:
courage, boldness, assurance, trust, certainty, unwavering

What other words, phrases or people come to mind when you think of the word *confidence*?

day 3

Immeasurably More *Confidence*

Today, you will read and reflect on some Bible stories that illustrate confidence in action.

PRAY God, speak to me through Your Word today. Reveal Yourself to me through these scriptures. Amen.

READ AND REFLECT Read each of these stories and write out the insights you discover about wisdom.

Joshua 1—A new leader urged to be strong and courageous

Judges 4—A prophet and judge confidently faces enemy armies

Acts 4:1–31—The Holy Spirit and boldness

In what area are you lacking confidence? What is one biblical truth you've learned that can help you in this area?

What is one thing you can do to apply godly confidence to the challenges or opportunities in your life?

"In him and through faith in him we may approach God with freedom and confidence."

EPHESIANS 3:12

Immeasurably More *Confidence*

Today, you will read this week's key verse and take steps to apply it to your life.

PRAY   God, speak to me through Your Word today. Reveal Yourself to me through these scriptures. Amen.

READ   Ephesians 3:12 (NIV). Want more insight? Read Ephesians 3:12 in more than one translation. See page 11. *Suggestions:* ESV, NLT, MSG

REFLECT   God speaks and reveals Himself to us through His Word. What does Ephesians 3:12 teach you about God?

What is one practical step you can take to apply this scripture to your life?

Use this space to reflect on what God spoke to you today and write out a prayer to Him.

Write out Ephesians 3:12 (NIV):

Have you memorized Ephesians 3:20-21 yet? Take a moment to write it out below:

Scripture Memorization Tip: To help you commit scripture to memory, write out this scripture on a sticky note or index card to post on your mirror or in your vehicle. See if you can recite the scripture you're commiting to memory the next time you meet with your eGroup.

confidence review

Something God revealed to me about confidence is:

One practical thing I plan to do to access immeasurably more confidence in my life is:

God, thank You for all the ways You've kept me. And it's because You've kept me that I know I can approach You confidently as the source of all my needs. Help me to replace my insecurities and fears with the confidence I can find in Your Word. In Jesus's name, **AMEN.**

Immeasurably More *Peace*

peace *n.*

1. harmony in personal relationship
2. freedom from strife or discord
3. a state of calm

group time

Earlier in Ephesians, Paul described the peace all followers of Jesus can know with God and with one another. This week, we will learn to pursue this peace by seeking to not only maintain but strengthen unity among each other.

Read Ephesians 4 out loud as a group, and jot down anything that stands out to you below.

video teaching notes

Share a time when someone assumed the best about you and how that impacted you.

Which of the three questions (Can you stay grounded? Am I assuming the best about this person? Am I willing to apologize first?) are the most difficult for you to put into practice in your everyday relationships?

BONUS: Who is one person in your life that you might need to begin the process of restoring peace with and what is one action step that you feel like God is calling you to take?

Father, today, rather than searching for peace as though it were some mystery, we're choosing to remind ourselves that Your Son, the Prince of Peace, has already made this promise to us and declared over us: "Peace I leave with you; my peace I give to you." Today, with Your help, we're choosing immeasurably more peace over the pressures swirling around us. Thank You, Father!

AMEN.

day 1   Immeasurably More *Peace*

Today, you will read scripture and begin to activate it in your life.

PRAY   God, speak to me through Your Word today. Reveal Yourself to me through these scriptures. Amen.

READ   Ephesians 4 — As you read your Bible, take time to focus on what the Lord is speaking to you through this chapter. Take note of, highlight, or underline what stands out to you in this week's reading, and be on the lookout for this week's theme: *peace*.

REFLECT   In your own words, what is peace to you?

What stood out to you about peace in this week's reading?

After reading chapter 4 of Ephesians, what else caught your attention from these scriptures?

The Word of God contains the keys to acquiring the peace we all seek. Each day as you read, meditate, and act on what God is speaking to you, peace is being activated in your life, even through life's most challenging circumstances.

JOHN 16:33	Peace in trials
1 THESSALONIANS 5:23A	Peace through maturing
2 CORINTHIANS 13:11	Peace in relationships
GALATIANS 5:22–23	Peace in life
ROMANS 16:20	Peace for a victory

MORE PEACE

We all want to experience peace, but if we're honest, there are times when it seems impossible to obtain. There are things we allow to be barriers to peace with others, such as age, race, and political leanings. There are also things that disrupt our internal peace, such as comparison, insecurities, and stress. We ourselves even become barriers to peace when we allow such things to take precedence over God's promise for peace in our lives.

Ephesians 4:3 says to "Make every effort to keep the unity of the Spirit through the bond of peace." Paul's instruction to "make every effort" means we each have an active part to play in experiencing immeasurably more peace. Start today by placing your attention and mind on higher things, because when we allow God's Word to speak to our spirits, peace follows.

People of Ephesus: Apollos

GUARDING PEACE AND UNITY

One of the many people whose paths took them through Ephesus in the first century was the little-known but fascinating Bible figure of Apollos. Apollos was from Alexandria, an important city and center of learning and philosophy in Egypt. A member of the Jewish community there, Apollos had been well trained in the Hebrew scriptures (Old Testament). He also may have picked up the allegorical style of teaching that was associated with Alexandria in this era.

Somewhere along the way, Apollos heard about Jesus and became an enthusiastic Christian. Bold and fearless, he tried to persuade his fellow Jews in Ephesus that Jesus was the Messiah. Yet he was a part of a group of Jesus followers in Ephesus whose theology was incomplete. So the Christian couple Priscilla and Aquila filled Apollos in on what he had been missing (Acts 18:24–26).

Apollos moved on to the city of Corinth, where he became a much-appreciated preacher, teaching about Jesus to both Jews and Gentiles (Acts 18:27–28). However, in about AD 55, Paul wrote to the Corinthians, "One of you says, 'I follow Paul'; another, 'I follow Apollos'; another, 'I follow Cephas'; still another, 'I follow Christ'" (1 Corinthians 1:12). In other words, the church in Corinth was starting to split into factions, formed around different preferred leaders. This was a serious problem. Paul cried out, "Is Christ divided?" (verse 13).

Apollo's story, then, is a reminder that Jesus followers must always be on guard against threats to our peace and unity. Differences in things such as racial background or church preferences shouldn't disrupt the oneness given to us in Jesus.

day 2 Immeasurably More *Peace*

Today, you will read some of the Bible's important passages about peace and gain a broader understanding of this biblical concept.

PEACE

Peace in the NIV Bible: **249 mentions**
Peace in Ephesians: **7 mentions**
Ephesians 1:2; 2:14, 15, 17; 4:3; 6:15, 23

You may have heard the Hebrew word *shalom.* It means much more than just "hello." Although usually translated as "peace," *shalom* refers to wholeness, soundness, and well-being. People in Old Testament times realized peace on that level didn't really exist in any stable way. However, they looked forward to a time when it would. The messianic age was to be a time of supernatural peace (Isaiah 2:2-4; 11:1–9), with the Messiah as the Prince of Peace (9:6).

The New Testament's comparable term is *eirene.* Paul's standard greeting was "Grace and peace *[eirene]* to you" (Ephesians 1:2). This pairing of peace with grace reminds us of the true source of peace. The Messiah and Son of God—Jesus—brought about peace, not by leading Israel to peace on the world's political stage but by creating a means through which hearts could be changed. For Christians, peace starts with being reconciled with God through Christ's sacrifice for us (Romans 5:1). When we have peace with God, we can have peace with others and peace within ourselves.

The New Testament repeatedly reminds us that, because we have been forgiven by God, we should forgive others. Reconciliation with others is a goal whenever our relationships are disrupted—that's why "blessed are the peacemakers" (Matthew 5:9). Paul said, "If it is possible, as far as it depends on you, live at peace with everyone" (Romans 12:18).

The peace described in Ephesians 4 is specifically the union of believers in Christ. Paul probably had in mind the difficult relations between Jewish and Gentile followers of Jesus in his day (Ephesians 2:11—3:6). In any case, the temptation of division is never ending, and we must fight against it to preserve the unity of the Spirit.

Finally, peace is a feeling. It is one of the fruits of the Spirit (Galatians 5:22). By giving our cares over to God, we can know the peace that "transcends all understanding" (Philippians 4:7). It is possible to have untroubled hearts even in the middle of discord (John 14:27; 16:33).

PRAY   God, speak to me through Your Word today. Reveal Yourself to me through these scriptures. Amen.

READ   Matthew 5:21–26—Conflict and resolution
                  Romans 5:1–11—The theology of peace with God
                  1 Timothy 2:1–7—Living peaceful lives

REFLECT   What are some cultural definitions of peace you've heard that you would say are off after gaining a
                  broader biblical understanding of this concept?

                  What truths about peace did you discover that you want to remember?

Many Gifts, One Goal

Paul set before the Ephesians the goal of maintaining "the unity of the Spirit through the bond of peace" (4:3). How does that actually work? One key part of it is the way God set up church leadership.

Christians have unity in the Spirit and yet a diversity of spiritual gifts. That diversity is demonstrated in both manifestations (such as healing and speaking in tongues) and ministries (different roles in the church). In Ephesians 4:11, the apostle Paul mentioned five ministry roles from his day: "Christ himself gave the apostles, the prophets, the evangelists, the pastors and teachers."

1. *Apostles* means "sent ones." The apostles were Jesus's original twelve disciples, plus Paul. These men had the primary authority to establish the true doctrine of the gospel, which gradually became embodied in the New Testament. The apostles traveled widely and led in the spread of the church.

2. The *prophets* received and passed on messages from the Holy Spirit for the guidance and building up of others. Unlike people who spoke in tongues, prophets spoke in intelligible language (1 Corinthians 14). The book of Acts records one occasion when a prophet had a message for Paul himself (21:10–11).

3. The word *evangelists* comes from *evangel*, meaning "good news" or "gospel," so the evangelists were people specially gifted in proclaiming the gospel. Like the apostles, the evangelists in the early church seem to have traveled widely. Philip and his daughters were evangelists (Acts 8:4–8; 21:8–9).

4. The word *pastors* means "shepherds." These local church leaders—also called "overseers" and "elders" in the New Testament—looked after the church like shepherds looked after their sheep.

5. *Teachers* were closely related to the pastors. In fact, they may have been the same group. These were people who took the lead in teaching the scriptures and Christian beliefs within a local church.

The message is clear for today: Bring your gifts to the table! We need all of them to tie the church together in peace and bring it to Christlikeness.

peace

synonyms:
calm, accord, kindness, tranquility, harmony, amicable

What other words, phrases or people come to mind when you think of the word *peace*?

Immeasurably More *Peace*

Today, you will read and reflect on some Bible stories that illustrate different types of peace.

PRAY   God, speak to me through Your Word today. Reveal Yourself to me through these scriptures. Amen.

READ AND REFLECT   Read each of these stories and write out the insights you discover about peace.

Mark 4:35–41—Jesus brought peace to nature and to the disciples' hearts

Acts 9:1–31—A persecutor of Jesus was given peace with Jesus

Genesis 32–33—Jacob established peace with his brother

In what area are you lacking peace? What is one biblical truth you've learned that can help you in this area?

What is one thing you can do to apply godly peace to the challenges or opportunities in your life?

"Be completely humble and gentle; be patient, bearing with one another in love. Make every effort to keep the unity of the Spirit through the bond of peace."

EPHESIANS 4:2–3

day 4 Immeasurably More *Peace*

Today, you will read this week's key verses and take steps to apply them to your life.

PRAY   God, speak to me through Your Word today. Reveal Yourself to me through these scriptures. Amen.

READ   Ephesians 4:2–3 (NIV). Want more insight? Read Ephesians 4:2–3 in more than one translation. See page 11. *Suggestions:* ESV, NLT, MSG

REFLECT   God speaks and reveals Himself to us through His Word. What does Ephesians 4:2–3 teach you about God?

What is one practical step you can take to apply this scripture to your life?

Use this space to reflect on what God spoke to you today and write out a prayer to Him.

Write out Ephesians 4:2–3:

Take a moment to write out Ephesians 3:20-21 from memory:

Scripture Memorization Tip: To help you commit scripture to memory, download an app for that purpose, such as the Bible Memory App. Use this tool through the week and see if you can recite the scripture you're commiting to memory the next time you meet with your eGroup.

peace review

Something God revealed to me about peace is:

One practical thing I plan to do to access immeasurably more peace in my life is:

God, thank You for Your peace that surpasses all understanding. I ask You to help me recall the peace You've promised me in every circumstance when I need it most. Seal this promise on my heart. In Jesus's name. **AMEN.**

Immeasurably More *Love*

love *n.*

1. strong affection, desire and devotion
2. an unconditional commitment to seek the
greatest good for another

love *v.*

1. a sacrificial action

group time

We will never fully understand the immeasurable love of God. He loves us so much that He sacrificed His one and only Son for us. This week, in chapter 5 of Ephesians, Paul shares how much Jesus loves us, and we have a responsibility to share that love with others.

Read Ephesians 5 out loud as a group, and jot down anything that stands out to you below.

video teaching notes

On a scale of 1–10, how much do you feel like you are a beloved child of God and why?

What is one practical way you can keep God's love in front of you at all times?

Father, You call us Your dearly loved children, which means You have a special kind of love for us. It's a love that is immeasurably greater than that of any earthly father. It's not a warm feeling toward us but a love that always does what is best for us—a love demonstrated supremely in the giving of Your Son, Jesus, on our behalf. Help us every day to imitate that love by loving ourselves like You love us and loving others like You love them. AMEN.

day 1   Immeasurably More *Love*

Today, you will read scripture and begin to activate it in your life.

PRAY   God, speak to me through Your Word today. Reveal Yourself to me through these scriptures. Amen.

READ   Ephesians 5 — As you read your Bible, take time to focus on what the Lord is speaking to you through this chapter. Take note of, highlight, or underline what stands out to you in this week's reading, and be on the lookout for this week's theme: *love*.

REFLECT   In your own words, what is love to you?

What stood out to you about love in this week's reading?

After reading chapter 5 of Ephesians, what else caught your attention from these scriptures?

This week's chapter charges us to walk in love—but what does that mean? Walking in love does not mean we simply *feel* for people but that we *do* for people. 1 John 3:18 says we must love in both our deeds and our words. When we love in a way that follows Jesus's example, we practice the type of love that can change a home, a workplace, a marriage, a family, or even the world by allowing God to love others through you.

Ways to walk in love:

PROVERBS 17:1	Respond without arguing.
2 CORINTHIANS 9:7	Give willingly.
JAMES 1:19	Speak without accusing.
COLOSSIANS 1:9	Pray for others.
PHILIPPIANS 2:3	Be selfless.
PROVERBS 15:1	Exercise kindness.
COLOSSIANS 3:13	Forigve others.
2 PETER 1:5–7	Exercise self-control.
PROVERBS 18:6–8	Do not gossip.

MORE LOVE

In chapter 5, Paul gave us handles on how we should live, and he shared the key ingredient to this: *love*. Love means different things to different people. Some people see love as a strong feeling for another person, while others may simply see it as a checkbox or an event. But we learned the love Paul wrote about is so much more than that. It is a way of life and a continual expression of selflessness, sacrifice, and action.

God is the source of this type of love, and you are the vessel He's seeking to fill and work through. He's blessed you with every spiritual blessing; He's called you holy and blameless; He's adopted you and forgiven you and chosen you and sacrificed His most precious gift for you. Being an open vessel means accepting the immeasurable amount of love God has for you so that love can overflow from you to others.

People of Ephesus: John

THE ONE JESUS LOVED

The Bible contains no mention of the apostle John living in Ephesus, and yet—with the exception of Paul—John may be the Christian leader who has been most closely associated with Ephesus.

If the apostle John was the same John who wrote the book of Revelation (widely believed to be the case), that means the apostle John spent time in exile on the island of Patmos, not far from Ephesus (Revelation 1:9). The book of Revelation is addressed to the church of Ephesus and six other churches in the same area (1:4; 2–3). According to historical reports dating back at least to the second century, John founded the church in Ephesus that Paul visited and strengthened, and later, John returned to the city to live out the rest of his days.

Although Jesus teased John and his brother by calling them "sons of thunder" because of their eagerness to call down fire from heaven to destroy their enemies (Mark 3:17; Luke 9:54), John went on to become closely associated with love. It is his gospel that says, "God so loved the world..." (John 3:16) and records Jesus' words about a new command to love one another (13:34). It is his letter that tells us God is love (1 John 4:8).

In the gospel he wrote John never referred to himself by name. Instead, he called himself "the disciple whom Jesus loved" (John 13:23; 19:26; 20:2; 21:7, 20). This choice was probably motivated by humility; instead of identifying himself by name as a participant in many of the great events of Jesus' life, he remained anonymous, just a follower of Jesus loved by God. In fact, all followers of Jesus are ones whom Jesus loves.

John is believed to have been buried in Ephesus, and a church was built on the site of his grave.

A memory about John recorded by the theologian Jerome in 386 may or may not have a basis in historical fact. Nevertheless, it captures John's commitment to the Christian virtue of love. Jerome wrote,

> The blessed John the Evangelist lived in Ephesus until extreme old age. His disciples could barely carry him to church and he could not muster the voice to speak many words. During individual gatherings he usually said nothing but, "Little children, love one another." The disciples and brothers in attendance, annoyed because they always heard the same words, finally said, "Teacher, why do you always say this?" He replied with a line worthy of John: "Because it is the Lord's commandment and if it alone is kept, it is sufficient."

What do you think John meant by saying it's enough if we keep the commandment of love? Do you agree?

day 2 Immeasurably More *Love*

Today, you will read some of the Bible's important passages about love and gain a broader understanding of this biblical concept.

LOVE

Love in the NIV Bible: **686 mentions**
Love in Ephesians: **17 mentions**
Ephesians 1:4, 6, 15; 2:4; 3:17–19; 4:2, 15–16; 5:1–2, 25, 28, 33; 6:23–24

Love is the staple of our faith and the directive in the two greatest commandments: to love God above all, and to love your neighbor as you love yourself (Matthew 22:36–40).

Greek (the language used for the New Testament) had several words for love. Of these, *agape* [pronounced ah-GAH-pee] was one of the least frequently used in non-biblical writings. Yet in the New Testament, when we see the word "love," it almost always translates *agape*. Clearly this was a word the New Testament writers felt they needed to express the type of love that originates from God.

The word *agape* refers to loving the undeserving, despite disappointment and rejection. It is an unconditional love. This definition of love is particularly appropriate for Christ's love of us. We have done nothing to deserve the love He showed on the cross, yet He loves us anyway. Because of His example and His grace to us, we, too, can love others because God asks us to, regardless of whether others seem to deserve it.

PRAY   God, speak to me through Your Word today. Reveal Yourself to me through these scriptures. Amen.

READ   John 3:16—God's love for us
                  1 Corinthians 13—The many facets of love
                  1 John 4:7–21—We love because God first loved us

REFLECT   What are some cultural definitions of love you've heard that you would say are off after gaining a
                  broader biblical understanding of this concept?

                  What truths about love did you discover that you want to remember?

Household Codes

The apostles Paul and Peter both wrote about relationships within Christian households and within households of faith (local churches, which were based in private homes and operated like extended families). These instructions are called *household codes*, and in the New Testament they can be found in:

EPHESIANS
- **Ephesians 5:22-33:** wives and husbands
- **Ephesians 6:1–4:** children and parents
- **Ephesians 6:5–9:** slaves and masters

COLOSSIANS
- **Colossians 3:18–19:** wives and husbands
- **Colossians 3:20–21:** children and parents
- **Colossians 3:22–4:1:** slaves and masters

TITUS
- **Titus 2:2–8:** older and younger men, older and younger women
- **Titus 2:9–10:** slaves

1 TIMOTHY
- **1 Timothy 2:1–7:** the church and civil authorities
- **1 Timothy 2:8–15:** men and women
- **1 Timothy 3:1–7:** overseers
- **1 Timothy 3:8–13:** deacons
- **1 Timothy 5:1–2:** older and younger men, older and younger women
- **1 Timothy 5:3–16:** widows
- **1 Timothy 5:17–20:** elders
- **1 Timothy 6:1–2:** slaves and masters

1 PETER
- **1 Peter 2:13-17:** the church and civil authorities
- **1 Peter 2:18-25:** slaves
- **1 Peter 3:1-17:** wives and husbands

The household codes can raise questions about their application and meaning in today's world. What principles do they teach us about men's and women's roles? Who should occupy positions of leadership? What is the role of a citizen in society?

It can be easy to contextually misappropriate the meaning and instructions given through Paul and Peter's writings to readers today because of the differences in the social standards in Greco-Roman culture and modern Western culture. Notable facts of Greco-Roman culture:

- Society operated from a hierarchical worldview, with the lowest positions reserved for women, children and slaves.
- Women, children and slaves often went unaddressed and unacknowledged.
- Between 20 and 25 percent of persons were slaves at this time.

The New Testament's household codes were counter-cultural because they addressed those perceived to be in power positions and those with less power. Rather than investing all authority in one person, they emphasize how people in different roles are mutually responsible to one another, all of them under the authority of Christ.

While our identity is always attached to such things as race, status, and gender, these things mean nothing in comparison to one's identity in Christ. Paul said, "There is neither Jew nor Gentile, neither slave nor free, nor is there male and female, for you are all one in Christ Jesus" (Galatians 3:28). That was a radical principle in the first century—and it still is today!

Select one or two of the household codes to read. As you read, keep in mind the overarching truth that what God desires for our relationships is love and harmony in our homes and churches.

What can you take away and apply to your life? What questions do you still have?

If present-day implications of the household codes intrigue you, do further research on them, and consider going to coffee with a member of your group to discuss them further.

love

synonyms:
affection, empathy, intimacy, cherish, attachment, appreciation

What other words, phrases or people come to mind when you think of the word *love?*

day 3   Immeasurably More *Love*

Today, you will read and reflect on some Bible stories that illustrate different types of love.

PRAY

God, speak to me through Your Word today. Reveal Yourself to me through these scriptures. Amen.

READ AND REFLECT

Read each of these stories and write out the insights you discover about love.

Ruth 1—Ruth's love for Naomi, representing our love for our dear ones

Luke 10:25–37—A Samaritan's love for an injured Jew, representing our love for strangers and enemies

Luke 15:11–32—A father's love for his prodigal son, representing God's love for us

In what area are you lacking love? What is one biblical truth you've learned that can help you in this area?

What is one thing you can do to apply godly love to the challenges or opportunities in your life?

"Follow God's example, therefore, as dearly loved children and walk in the way of love, just as Christ loved us and gave himself up for us as a fragrant offering and sacrifice to God."

EPHESIANS 5:1–2

 **day 4** Immeasurably More *Love*

Today, you will read this week's key verses and take steps to apply them to your life.

PRAY   God, speak to me through Your Word today. Reveal Yourself to me through these scriptures. Amen.

READ   Ephesians 5:1–2 (NIV). Want more insight? Read Ephesians 5:1–2 in more than one translation.
              See page 11. *Suggestions:* ESV, NLT, MSG

REFLECT   God speaks and reveals Himself to us through His Word. What does Ephesians 5:1–2 teach you
              about God?

What is one practical step you can take to apply this scripture to your life?

Use this space to reflect on what God spoke to you today and write out a prayer to Him.

Write out Ephesians 5:1–2 (NIV):

Take a moment to write out Ephesians 3:20-21 from memory:

Scripture Memorization Tip: To help you commit scripture to memory, write it on a whiteboard or piece of paper. Keep repeating it, erasing one word per repetition, until you can speak the entire passage without reading it. See if you can recite the scripture you're commiting to memory the next time you meet with your eGroup.

love review

Something God revealed to me about love is:

One practical thing I plan to do to access immeasurably more love in my life is:

God, help me to not just read about the immeasurable amount of love You have given me but also accept it and walk in it. I thank You for seeing me and loving me so graciously and fully, and I pray in return I can love others out of an overflow of all You've given to me. In Jesus's name,

AMEN.

Immeasurably More *Strength*

strength *n.*

1. the capacity of an object or substance to withstand great force or pressure

2. the quality or state of being strong

3. capacity for endurance

group time

In chapter 6 of Ephesians, we learn we should rely not on our own strength alone but also on the immeasurable strength of God to achieve victory in life's battles. This week, we'll learn that when we are rooted in God, we are able to withstand the challenges of life and come out victorious.

Read Ephesians 6 out loud as a group, and jot down anything that stands out to you below.

video teaching notes

Share an example of how you've gotten stronger over the past six weeks.

What can you do to continue to get stronger after our time together is over?

Father, so often when we're facing the difficulties and challenges life brings, we're quick to think we don't have the strength to get through them. And the truth is, we don't—not on our own. Which is why You remind us in Your Word to be strong in You and Your power, not in ourselves. Your strength is not only enough, it's immeasurably more than enough. And we thank You that You make it accessible through our relationship with You.

AMEN.

day 1 Immeasurably More *Strength*

Today, you will read scripture and begin to activate it in your life.

PRAY   God, speak to me through Your Word today. Reveal Yourself to me through these scriptures. Amen.

READ   Ephesians 5 — As you read your Bible, take time to focus on what the Lord is speaking to you through this chapter. Take note of, highlight, or underline what stands out to you in this week's reading, and be on the lookout for this week's theme: *strength*.

REFLECT   In your own words, what is strength to you?

What stood out to you about strength in this week's reading?

After reading chapter 6 of Ephesians, what else caught your attention from these scriptures?

This week's chapter tells us to be strong in the Lord, but the word *strong* can be misleading. When we think of strength, we usually associate it with physical power. There are, however, many non-physical aspects of strength. When life gets difficult, it takes more than physical strength to stay grounded and prevent you from retreating and giving up. How much you can squat or bench press has no correlation to how you make it to the other side of suffering, loss, and hardship. We can only be so strong in *ourselves*. God knows this, and in response, He commands us to be strong in *Him*. True strength comes from recognizing our need to depend on God.

Meditate on these scriptures as a source of strength:

2 CORINTHIANS 4:8–9	You've already been promised victory.
ISAIAH 41:10	God will help you.
PHILIPPIANS 4:13	All things are possible through God.
ISAIAH 12:1–2	God is your strength.
JOSHUA 1:9	God is with you.
ROMANS 8:31–39	You are more than a conqueror.

MORE STRENGTH

Over the past few weeks, we have read the book of Ephesians and looked at the various ways Paul encouraged the church of Ephesus and the surrounding churches. Paul has helped us establish our relationship and standing with Jesus, and walked us through the basics of living a Christian life. The last section of this letter taught us how to sustain that walk, even when it's difficult, by teaching us to exercise the spiritual strength we have access to through Christ.

We've been gifted God's immeasurable strength through our relationship with Him. Through His strength, we can face life's most difficult challenges and come out victorious on the other side.

People of Ephesus: Mary

A MOTHER'S STRENGTH

If you go to the ruins of Ephesus today, a tour guide will be glad to show you an attractive stone building that is claimed to be the last home of Mary the mother of Jesus. Did Mary really live in Ephesus, either in this building or some other? It's possible.

According to John 19:26–27, while hanging on the cross, Jesus gave over the care of His mother to the apostle John. "From that time on, this disciple took her into his home." So *if* John lived in Ephesus at some point, and *if* Mary was still living at that time, then she presumably would have been in Ephesus with John. We can't, however, be sure. The earliest known historical references to Mary living in Ephesus date back only to the 300s. And the evidence is at least as strong that Mary lived out her last years and died in Jerusalem, where today you can visit

a building known as the Tomb of Mary. Wherever Mary lived, she remains a figure of strength we can admire today.

Perhaps her finest moment came when she was still a teenager, at the time when an angel gave her God's call to become the virgin mother of the Messiah. The angel promised, "For nothing will be impossible with God" (Luke 1:37 ESV). Yet the task was still scary. Mary submitted, saying, "I am the Lord's servant... May your word to me be fulfilled" (v. 38 NIV).

In time, she would have to call on every bit of strength as she kept vigil with her Son while He suffered and died. But she had her reward when she saw Jesus risen from the dead to live forevermore. Truly, nothing is impossible with God.

day 2 Immeasurably More *Strength*

Today, you will read some of the Bible's important passages about strength and gain a broader understanding of this biblical concept.

STRENGTH

Strength in the NIV Bible: **232 mentions**
Strength in Ephesians: **3 mentions**
Ephesians 1:19; 3:16; 6:10

God displays His strength all throughout scripture:

God showed His strength in creation when He spoke the heavens and earth into existence.

God showed His strength over nature when made the sun stand still, calmed the wind and the waves, and plagued Egypt when Pharaoh wouldn't let God's people go.

God showed His strength through redemption when He sent His Son to die and then destroyed death and sin by raising Him from the dead.

When Paul wrote, "Be strong in the Lord and in his mighty power" (Ephesians 6:10), he was using a version of the Greek word *dunamis*, usually translated as "strength" or "power." To the ancient Greeks, *dunamis* wasn't just a capacity; it was a major cosmic principle. Some Greek philosophers considered it to be second in importance only to nous (mind).

It's interesting that, when Paul referred to Satan and the evil spirits, he used words like "rulers," "authorities," "powers of this dark world," and "spiritual forces of evil in the heavenly realms." This is describing a powerful cosmic realm—a kingdom of evil.

But compared to God's strength, evil's strength is as nothing. So when we are strong "in the Lord and in his mighty power," we are allying with a power that our spiritual enemies rightly fear.

PRAY   God, speak to me through Your Word today. Reveal Yourself to me through these scriptures. Amen.

READ   Isaiah 40:28–31—Renewing your strength
2 Corinthians 12:6–10—Power made perfect in weakness
1 Peter 5:8–11—Lion taming

REFLECT   What are some cultural definitions of strength you've heard that you would say are off after gaining a broader biblical understanding of this concept?

What truths about strength did you discover that you want to remember?

Arm Yourself

Paul's last major topic in his letter to the Ephesians was one designed to put steel in his readers' souls: "Be strong in the Lord and in the strength of his might" (6:10 ESV). He was talking about standing firm in the faith despite all the attacks of our enemies through such things as temptations, hardships, and persecution.

If we had human enemies, we would need physical armor and weaponry. But since our enemies are spiritual, we must have spiritual armor.

Deeply immersed in the Hebrew scriptures, Paul undoubtedly had Isaiah 11:4–5 and 59:17 in mind when he described the armor of God. In those verses, Isaiah described the Messiah's warfare gear, including a sash of faithfulness, a breastplate of righteousness, and a cloak of zeal. Paul used the same kinds of images to describe some of the things that can keep us safe in a spiritual attack: truth, righteousness, the gospel, faith, salvation, and the Word of God.

Paul didn't specifically identify prayer as a piece of the armor of God, but after talking about armor, he naturally moved into the topic of prayer. In light of that, let us pray and arm ourselves with the armor of God.

Lord, help me to arm myself with the armor You've graciously provided:

THE BELT OF TRUTH (Ephesians 6:14)
As I put on the belt of truth, I pray You will protect me from lies and deception and allow truth to guard my mind, heart, and lips.

THE BREASTPLATE OF RIGHTEOUSNESS (Ephesians 6:14)
I'm placing the breastplate of righteousness to protect my heart from temptations that are not from You and to remind me that I am righteous in Your sight.

THE SHOES OF PEACE (Ephesians 6:15)
Allow the shoes of peace to help me walk in the peace and freedom You promise me. Help me to stay firmly grounded in You throughout this day.

THE SHIELD OF FAITH (Ephesians 6:16)
May I take up the shield of faith when hardship and threats to my peace and trust in You attempt to distract me throughout my day. Help me to use those moments as fuel for my faith as I take You at Your word and believe You for the victory You've already promised me.

THE HELMET OF SALVATION (Ephesians 6:17)
I pray the helmet of salvation protects my mind and thoughts. Remind me that I am Your child and help me to recall I have been saved by grace and nothing can separate me from Your love.

THE SWORD OF THE SPIRIT (Ephesians 6:17)
Help me remember Your words and Your promises throughout my day, but especially in the moments when I need them most. Help me use the full power Your Word gives me to strike back at the enemy and demolish temptations and strongholds, just as Jesus Himself did.

Heavenly Father, thank You for the armor You've given me to stand firm through the trials of this world. I thank You because I don't have to fight alone, and I praise You because, through You, the victory is already mine. In Jesus's name, amen.

strength

synonyms:
powerful, mighty, force, toughness, endurance, resilience

What other words, phrases or people come to mind when you think of the word *strength?*

day 3   Immeasurably More *Strength*

Today, you will read and reflect on some Bible stories that illustrate different types of strength.

PRAY God, speak to me through Your Word today. Reveal Yourself to me through these scriptures. Amen.

READ AND REFLECT Read each of these stories and write out the insights you discover about strength.

Judges 16:4–31—Samson's strength was lost and then restored

1 Samuel 17—The strength of a boy to accept a giant's challenge

Esther 4; 7:1–6—A queen showed great strength by risking her life for her people

In what area are you lacking strength? What is one biblical truth you've learned that can help you in this area?

What is one thing you can do to apply godly strength to the challenges or opportunities in your life?

son a man will leave his wife, and
become one flesh. This is a profound
— but I am talking about Christ and
However, each one of you also
his wife as he loves himself
respect her husband
obey your parents
Honor
and in one body to rec-
new humanity out of the two
His purpose was to create
in his flesh the law with its commands
the dividing wall of hostility, by setting
rier, the
For he himself is our peace, who has made
the two groups one and has destroyed the bar-
brought near by the blood of Christ.
Jesus you who once were far away have been
without God in the world. But now in Christ

"Finally, be strong in the Lord and in the strength of his might. Put on the whole armor of God, that you may be able to stand against the schemes of the devil."

EPHESIANS 6:10–11 ESV

day 4 Immeasurably More *Strength*

Today, you will read this week's key verses and take steps to apply them to your life.

PRAY God, speak to me through Your Word today. Reveal Yourself to me through these scriptures. Amen.

READ Ephesians 6:10–11 (ESV). Want more insight? Read Ephesians 6:10–11 in more than one translation. See page 11. *Suggestions:* NIV, NLT, MSG

REFLECT God speaks and reveals Himself to us through His Word. What does Ephesians 6:10–11 teach you about God?

What is one practical step you can take to apply this scripture to your life?

Use this space to reflect on what God spoke to you today and write out a prayer to Him.

Write out Ephesians 6:10–11 (ESV):

Take a moment to write out Ephesians 3:20-21 from memory:

Scripture Memorization Tip: To help you keep Ephesians scripture committed to memory, write down the first letter of each word in the verse. Use that to mentally repeat the verse during the day as frequently as you're able to until you have the verse committed to memory.

Revisit the scriptures from this study to secure them in your memory and heart.

strength review

Something God revealed to me about strength is:

One practical thing I plan to do to access immeasurably more strength in my life is:

God, thank You for how You strengthen and carry me. Help me to recall that, even in my weakest moments, You are strong. I thank You for providing all the strength I need to persevere through whatever I face in life. In Jesus's name, **AMEN.**

Personal Reflection

I did this Bible study from _____/_____/_____ *to* _____/_____/_____.

Things that were going on in my life at the time included:

My favorite part of the Ephesians letter is the part about:

Something God revealed to me during this Bible study that I never want to forget is:

Prayer requests from my group that I want to keep bringing to the Lord include:

Acknowledgments

Pastor Steven, thank you for creating a church where we can come from any background or place in our walk with God and still be welcomed and given the opportunity to grow in our faith. Thank you for sharing your God-given calling, gifts, and creativity with the world and for allowing us to follow suit and see what God can do through us.

To all of our **Elevation eGroup Leaders**, this study has no Impact without *YOU*. Thank you for creating opportunities for people to experience Jesus and grow in their faith through community.

———

To everyone who brought *Immeasurably More* to life, thank you for using your God-given gifts to reach people with the gospel. Through your gifts, people are learning to rely on God's Word and are opening their hearts to believe God for immeasurably more in their lives.

ART DIRECTION AND DESIGN
Sophie Smith

PROJECT MANAGEMENT
Heather Chamberlain, Aliscia Freitas, Ashley Hollingsworth

CONTENT AND EDITING
Gene Lakey, Mike Marshall

ARTWORK
Julius Shumpert

VIDEO
Dani Garcia, Brock Gregor, J. Cody Hall, Braden Kopf, Colten Marsh, Josh Meza, Alex Thomas

DIGITAL
Vinel Brown, Ida Goniche, Corey Pruitt, and the Digital Team

eGROUPS MINISTRY
Nick Falkowski, Jay Rabon and the eGroup Directors

SUPPORT
JT Akinsola, Ryan Hollingsworth

About the Creators

Holly Furtick and her husband, Steven, are the founders and pastors of Elevation Church, which launched in 2006 with the vision to see people far from God raised to life in Christ—and they have seen the church grow into a global ministry with multiple locations. Holly is the mother of Elijah, Graham and Abbey.

She holds a Bachelor of Arts degree in education from North Greenville University and is the author of multiple Bible studies, including "Building Friendships that Fit," "Becoming Mrs. Betterhalf," and "Essentials." She is passionate about using her gifts to see people find community and mature in their faith.

When she's not caring for her family or helping lead Elevation Church, Holly spends time reading, attempting to play tennis, or enjoying a cup of tea.

Follow her on Instagram @hollyfurtick, Facebook @hollyfurtick and YouTube Holly Furtick.

Brittany Akinsola is the wife of JT and mama to Eli. Brittany and her family live in Charlotte, North Carolina. She is the eGroups Pastor at Elevation Church. Brittany has been a part of Elevation Church for a decade and serves under the leadership of Pastor Steven and Holly Furtick. She has a passion to see the Bible come alive for people and to help others grow in their faith. She has led and been a part of several eGroups over the years and loves seeing God move in people's lives when they come together.

Aside from caring for her family and serving the ministry, Brittany also enjoys exploring new restaurants, traveling, and using her Bachelor of Science in nursing degree from the University of North Carolina at Charlotte to serve people in need all around the world.

———

Eric Stanford and his wife, Elisa, run a writing and editing studio called Edit Resource. He holds a bachelor's degree from Judson University and a master's degree in theology from Gordon-Conwell Theological Seminary.

Eric lives in the woods of Colorado with his wife and two teenage daughters, Eden and Elizabeth.